The Increase
in Leisure Inequality
1965–2005

The Increase
in Leisure Inequality
1965–2005

Mark Aguiar
and
Erik Hurst

The AEI Press

Publisher for the American Enterprise Institute

WASHINGTON, D.C.

Distributed to the Trade by National Book Network, 15200 NBN Way, Blue Ridge Summit, PA 17214. To order call toll free 1-800-462-6420 or 1-717-794-3800. For all other inquiries please contact the AEI Press, 1150 Seventeenth Street, N.W., Washington, D.C. 20036 or call 1-800-862-5801.

NRI NATIONAL RESEARCH INITIATIVE

This publication is a project of the National Research Initiative, a program of the American Enterprise Institute that is designed to support, publish, and disseminate research by university-based scholars and other independent researchers who are engaged in the exploration of important public policy issues.

Library of Congress Cataloging-in-Publication Data

Aguiar, Mark.
  The increase in leisure inequality, 1965-2005 / Mark Aguiar and Erik Hurst.
    p. cm.
  Includes bibliographical references.
  ISBN-13: 978-0-8447-4313-4
  ISBN-10: 0-8447-4313-5
  1. Leisure. 2. Equality. 3. Time—Sociological aspects. 4. Social classes—Time management. 5. Social values. I. Hurst, Erik. II. Title.

  HD4904.6.A35 2009
  306.4'812—dc22

                                        2009016981
13 12 11 10 09   1 2 3 4 5

Contents

List of Illustrations

Introduction

Which of the following two jobs is more desirable: (a) one that pays $75,000 a year for fifty hours of work per week, or (b) an identical job that pays $75,000 a year but requires only thirty hours per week? Clearly (b) is preferable, because it offers the same salary for considerably less time on the job. But now consider the following choice: (a) a job that pays $75,000 a year and requires fifty hours a week, or (b) an identical job that pays only $50,000 a year but requires only thirty hours a week. Here the answer is not obvious: some people might choose option (a), but others might still choose option (b), even though it now pays a lower salary. Why might the lower-paying option be perceived as more desirable? The answer is that people value not only monetary income but also their time, because time away from work (spending time with friends, listening to music, golfing, etc.) is assumed to be more enjoyable than time spent at work.

Much recent research has found that the trend in earnings for workers with relatively little education has been much lower than the trend in earnings for more highly educated workers (see Katz and Autor 1999; Attanasio and Davis 1996; Krueger and Perri 2006). However, little research has been devoted to measuring trends in leisure time across these groups. To gauge an individual's true well-being, we need to measure both that individual's income (which can be used to fund consumption) and the time he or she allocates to leisure. As the example above illustrated, time in and of itself has value to individuals, holding income constant.

In this monograph we document trends in the allocation of time by individuals in the United States over a recent forty-year period, paying particular attention to two separate questions. First, how did the amount of leisure time change for the average individual between 1965 and 2005? Second, how did the amount of leisure time change across groups with different levels of education over this same period, and to what extent are these changes explained by changing educational differences in employment status? With respect to the second question, although the wages of low-income groups increased less than those of higher-income groups from 1985 to 2005, we show that time spent on leisure activities has increased much more for the former than for the latter. Such findings are important in interpreting overall changes in the well-being of low-income groups during the last two decades.

To further preview our results, in the first part of our monograph we find that during this forty-year period, time spent in leisure increased for the average individual. We define leisure to include the following set of activities: watching television, socializing with friends and family, exercising and playing sports, reading, participating in hobbies and other entertainment, eating, sleeping, and engaging in personal care.[1] Below we document that our focal measure of leisure increased by over three hours per week for women from 1965 to 2005, to a total of 150.1 hours per week. For men, leisure increased by nearly five hours per week over this period, to a total of 106.2 hours per week. However, almost all of these gains in leisure occurred before 1985. Since 1985, leisure has been roughly constant for men and has declined for women.

In the second part of the monograph, we report findings indicating that leisure inequality has increased in the United States during the last forty years. We define leisure inequality as the difference in average time spent in leisure across people with different levels of education. Before 1985, average time spent in leisure was roughly comparable for men with different levels of schooling. After 1985, however, a significant educational "leisure gap" developed among men. For example, between 1985 and 2005, men who had not completed high school increased their leisure time by eight hours per week, while men who had completed college decreased their leisure time by six hours per week.

During the same period, the employment rate for less-educated men (defined in the rest of this monograph as those with a high school diploma or less) fell significantly relative to that of more-educated men (all others). This finding raises the important question of whether the observed growth in leisure inequality reflects increased involuntary unemployment (or disability) on the part of less-educated men. To explore this possibility, we answer the following four questions:

(1) For men who are working full time, does the allocation of time differ by educational attainment in 1985 and in the early 2000s?

(2) How do men who do not work, regardless of education, allocate the hours they would have spent working for pay?

(3) Do differences in education level affect how unemployed, disabled, and other nonemployed individuals (including homemakers and other individuals outside of the labor force) allocate their time, and did these relationships change over the period in question?

(4) How much of the increased leisure experienced by less-educated individuals over the last twenty years can be explained by changes in their employment status?

We find that within each broad employment status category (i.e., working versus nonworking) in 1985, men of different educational attainments exhibit similar time allocation patterns. However, this uniformity is not present in the early 2000s. In this period, for example, hours spent in market work (i.e., time spent working for pay) were similar for employed men regardless of their education, but less-educated employed men enjoyed four more hours of leisure per week than more-educated employed men. This four-hour gap exists because less-educated employed men performed less non-market work (e.g., cooking and cleaning in one's own home, shopping for groceries, doing laundry, doing yard work, maintaining the home) and less child care (taking care of one's own children) and engaged less in religious and civic activities. Even more striking is the finding that less-educated *nonemployed* men enjoyed ten more hours per week of leisure than more-educated nonemployed men. This gap exists because less-educated nonemployed men performed less "informal market work" (e.g., preparing food or drink for sale, making furniture for sale, playing in a band for pay, babysitting for pay, doing other household chores for pay, doing yard work or home and vehicle maintenance for pay) and engaged in less job search and training, in addition to participating less in nonmarket work, child care, and religious and civic activities.

In examining the sources of these large gaps in leisure time between more- and less-educated men, we find that roughly 30 percent of the difference in the 2003–2005 period is due to differences in employment status. The remaining 70 percent is explained by the fact that less-educated individuals enjoyed more leisure within all employment status categories. That is, whether they were unemployed or retired or disabled, less-educated men enjoyed more leisure than their more-educated counterparts. Additionally, we find that two-thirds of the increase in leisure among less-educated men between 1985 and 2003–2005 is due to changes in their employment status during this period. The decline in leisure that more-educated men experienced during this period, however, cannot be attributed to changes in their employment status. On net, less than half of the increase in leisure inequality can be attributed to trends in employment rates.

The remainder of the monograph is organized as follows:[2]

- Chapter 1 explains why we believe it is important to examine the changing nature of time allocation; we also define important terms, discuss the data sources used, and address relevant measurement issues.

- Chapter 2 reviews overall trends from 1965 to the early 2000s in how men and women allocate their time.

- Chapter 3 focuses on how the leisure gap has changed for men depending on their educational attainment. This chapter also presents a new set of facts about how nonemployed individuals allocate their time differently than their employed counterparts.

- Chapter 4 presents our analysis of how much of the difference in leisure by education level and the changing leisure gap since 1985 can be explained by differences in the employment rates of individuals with different levels of education.

- Chapter 5 presents some caveats and discusses how to relate our results to the broader issue of changing economic inequality.

1

Motivation and Methodology

This monograph seeks to understand why the allocation of time has evolved differently for individuals of differing educational attainment. First, however, it is worth explaining why time allocation is important and how it may influence our understanding of other economic phenomena. This discussion also helps frame the patterns documented in the rest of the monograph. After that discussion, we describe the data used in our analysis.

The Importance of Time Allocation

The starting point in understanding the importance of time allocation is to recognize that time is a component of nearly every economic undertaking. Naturally, time is an indispensable element of market labor. Individuals get compensated for allocating their time to employers in return for wages. However, time is also a key input into individual consumption, as argued by Becker (1965). According to Becker, individuals consume a range of different consumption goods (referred to as consumption "commodities"). Each commodity is produced with a combination of one or more household members' time and tangible inputs, using a production technology. For example, the inputs needed for a meal (a consumption commodity) likely include ingredients bought in the market, time spent shopping for the ingredients, time spent cooking, and time spent eating. Similarly, watching a sporting event on television involves the services of a television set as well as the time spent watching the event. In Becker's model, market labor is just one of many uses of time that ultimately produce consumption commodities.

Viewed in this way, the standard dichotomy between market work and "leisure," a catch-all term, does not distinguish whether time is allocated to cooking, watching television, volunteering at the local food pantry, or attending meetings of one's church's finance committee. Why is it important to make such distinctions? One reason is that because economics is the study of how agents allocate scarce resources, the allocation of time (a very scarce resource for most people) is interesting in and of itself.

Second, and potentially more important, if we want to understand why people offer their labor in the market, and how changes in market wages affect how much labor they offer, we need to understand how time away from the market is allocated. If take-home wages increase (perhaps as a result of a tax cut) and individuals as a consequence choose to work more hours, are they more likely to substitute that time away from home production (e.g., cooking) or from leisure properly defined (e.g., watching television)? What happens to labor supply in the market when there are innovations in home production technology (e.g., microwave ovens or vacuum cleaners)? What happens to market labor supply where there are innovations in leisure technology (e.g., high-definition television or the Internet)?

Understanding how increases in market wages and improvements in home production technology and leisure technology affect how much time people allocate to market work depends both on their existing use of time and on the elasticity of substitution between time and goods used in the production of the different consumption commodities. For example, a higher wage might allow someone to make additional market expenditures (e.g., buy a microwave or order takeout food) in order to reduce the time input associated with preparing a meal. The additional expenditure reduces the time that must be allocated to meal preparation, allowing more time to be allocated to market work, if the individual desires. But market expenditures cannot significantly reduce the time input to watching television (although innovations like VCRs and DVRs allow some substitution by allowing one to fast-forward, skip commercials, and so on). In economic terms, there is a high elasticity of substitution between market expenditures and time devoted to the production of a meal (a home-produced good), but a low elasticity of substitution between market expenditures and time devoted to the production of television watching (a leisure good).

Decades ago, Reid (1934) argued that leisure activities are those activities that generate utility from the "doing" itself. Take again the distinction between preparing a meal and watching television. Our framework extends Reid's definition by defining ease of substitutability between one's own time and market-purchased inputs in producing the consumption good as the crucial characteristic in identifying "leisure": leisure activities are those for which such substitution is relatively difficult. Note that this implies that one can potentially rank activities along a continuum (ordered by the technological elasticity of substitution), with no clear-cut dividing line between "leisure" and "home production."

Moreover, the existence of a market for an activity does not necessarily indicate an activity's leisure content. For example, although one can purchase child care on the market (e.g., by hiring a nanny), it is not obvious that the ultimate consumption commodity is the same whether the time allocated to child care is supplied by a parent or by a hired market substitute. On the one hand, the commodities needed to make a clean, well-nourished child seem amenable to market purchase (a nanny can feed and bathe a child). On the other hand, the bond between parent and child resulting from time together cannot be purchased on the market. Whether child care is leisure or home production depends on how we view the parental consumption commodity of "children." In other words, is spending time with one's children work or leisure? In the case of child care, as with many other activities, the answer is not obvious.

As touched on above, an important aspect of how the allocation of time away from market work affects market outcomes is the effect on market labor supply. In Becker's model, whether a wage increase draws a worker into market work depends not only on how much the worker likes consumption commodities or how much the worker dislikes working, but also on how easy it is to substitute expenditure for time in creating the consumption commodities. If individuals are engaged in activities that have a high degree of substitutability between goods and time, they will supply labor to the market differently in response to a wage increase than will agents engaged in activities that have a low elasticity of substitution.

For example, suppose an individual who spends a significant amount of time on home production is offered market employment at a certain wage. Given the ease of finding market substitutes for home production, it should take only a small increase in the wage to draw the individual into the work force. This generates a very elastic labor supply response. That is, if wages rise by 3 percent, the individual's labor supply might rise by 3 percent or even more. This high elasticity of labor supply with respect to wages is consistent with the fact that rising market wages for women and declines in the price of goods used in home production accompanied an increase in female labor force participation in the twentieth century (see Greenwood, Seshadri, and Yorukoglu 2005). Conversely, if employment means forgoing an activity that cannot be purchased in the market, whether it be watching television or playing golf, it may take a large wage increase to generate a 3 percent increase in labor supply.

These examples show that how agents allocate their time away from the market has a direct bearing on our understanding of market labor supply. Such an accounting of time allocation may also guide our understanding of why labor supply elasticities change over time and across demographic and other groups, why hours and employment vary, and how technological shocks in the production of home-produced goods or in the production of market goods influence total output.

Moreover, understanding time allocation is important in distinguishing a household's actual "consumption" from its market expenditure. In previous work (Aguiar and Hurst 2005, 2007b) we have documented that simply looking at what households spend provides a misleading picture of their true consumption. For example, much research has shown that food expenditure tends to decline at retirement. This decline has been viewed as evidence that retirees suffer from their own poor planning: having failed to save enough during their working years, they must now curtail their consumption. As our previous work shows, however, such conclusions were flawed because they failed to account for how households allocate their time away from market work. We documented that the time retirees spend shopping and cooking increases dramatically at the same time that they are reducing their expenditure at the grocery store. Part of the decline in expenditure by retirees is due to the lower prices they pay as a result of intensive shopping for bargains. Similarly, by preparing more of their own food, retirees can forgo more expensive prepared foods and buy the raw ingredients instead. That is, retirees can substitute their time for market expenditures on food. Food diaries indicate that the average retiree's actual food intake does not decline, even though spending on food in the grocery store declines sharply. This finding provides just one example of the importance of time allocation in understanding market outcomes.

More generally, taking time allocation into consideration is important if we are to make correct inferences about individual well-being. For example, the well-documented increase in the wages and expenditures of more-educated individuals relative to those of less-educated individuals (Katz and Autor 1999; Attanasio and Davis 1996; Krueger and Perri 2006) has been accompanied by little change in the relative time spent in home production but a large change in the relative time spent in leisure. In chapter 5 we return to the question of how such time allocation can inform discussions about the welfare consequences of wage, income, and expenditure inequality.

Methodology

Three types of surveys provide useful data for measuring time allocation. The first is the standard household survey such as the U.S. Bureau of Labor Statistics' Current Population Survey (CPS) or the University of Michigan's Panel Study of Income Dynamics (PSID). Respondents to such surveys typically report the market hours worked in a typical week (also called the reference week) and the market weeks worked per year. Again, we refer to market work as the time individuals spend working for pay. These surveys have two drawbacks in measuring time allocation. The first is that the focus is only on market work, with little or no reporting of other uses of time. The second is that respondents may not have a precise idea of their typical workweek or of the number of weeks they worked in a previous year.

The second type of survey collects data on one's immediate activity. For example, in the ecological momentary assessment (EMA) methodology popular with psychologists and medical clinicians, respondents use an electronic device that prompts them at random times during the day to record their activities and answer questions on stress levels, emotional state, pain symptoms, and so on. Although this method avoids the errors that arise from faulty memory, the samples must be very large to obtain accurate coverage of time allocation for a twenty-four-hour period.

The third type of survey, and the source of the data used in this monograph and in most other recent time allocation studies, involves the keeping of time diaries. These surveys offer the best approach for measuring time allocation across a number of activities as well as over a significant time frame. The typical time diary survey works as follows. Individuals are contacted at random and asked about how they spent their time the previous day. For example, respondents might be asked to report all activities in fifteen-minute intervals over a twenty-four-hour period. The focus on the previous day mitigates some of the poor recall issues of standard household surveys. The diaries also deter overreporting of certain activities, such as market work, because the sum of all activities cannot exceed twenty-four hours.

This monograph uses data gathered from three time diary surveys: the 1965–1966 Americans' Use of Time survey; the 1985 version of the same survey; and the American Time Use Surveys (ATUS) of 2003, 2004, and 2005. The data appendix to this monograph describes these surveys in some detail. Each survey is based on twenty-four-hour time diaries. Survey personnel assign each reported activity to a category in a predetermined classification scheme. The more refined the classification scheme, the less the survey needs to rely on the judgment of surveyors in correctly coding activities. The

ATUS represents the state of the art of time use surveys for the United States and reports 406 detailed time use categories. The earlier surveys used schemes of slightly fewer than 100 categories. For our research we aggregate the detailed survey categories into a small number of broader categories. As we have constructed the categories, they are mutually exclusive, and they sum to the household's entire day. In other words, each person in the survey has twenty-four hours of nonoverlapping activities. Note that throughout this monograph, time spent on an activity includes any time spent on transportation associated with that activity. Our major time aggregates, which will be the focus of our analysis, are the following.

Total market work includes all time spent working for pay in the formal market sector on main jobs, second jobs, and overtime, as well as time spent commuting to and from work, time spent on work-related meals and activities, time spent searching for a job, and time spent working for pay in the informal sector.[3] The last category includes any activities for which an individual earns income by working in the informal sector, such as babysitting for pay, doing home improvements for pay, doing household chores for pay, selling items at a flea market, and so on. When noted, we separate from total market work the time spent on *job search*. This adjustment allows us to study the extent to which unemployed and disabled individuals spend time looking for employment.

Total nonmarket work consists of three subcategories: home and vehicle maintenance; obtaining goods and services (i.e., shopping); and all other home production. Time spent on *home and vehicle maintenance* includes any time spent cleaning or repairing home exteriors or vehicles. Examples include painting home exteriors, building a deck, cleaning a garage, shoveling snow, building a bird feeder, changing vehicle oil, restoring a car, washing a car, and repairing a car. Time spent *obtaining goods and services* includes all time spent acquiring goods or services (excluding medical care, education, and restaurant meals). Examples include grocery shopping, shopping for other household items, comparison shopping, coupon clipping, going to the bank, going to the post office, and buying goods online. *All other home production* includes, among other things, any time spent on meal preparation and cleanup, doing laundry, ironing, dusting, vacuuming, indoor household cleaning, and indoor design and maintenance (including indoor painting and decorating).

We treat *child care* as a separate time use category. Total time spent in child care combines time spent caring for a child's physical needs (breastfeeding, changing diapers, etc.), teaching a child (reading to a child, disciplining a child, attending parent-teacher conferences, etc.), and playing with a child (including watching a child participate in sporting events). Another separate time category is *gardening, lawn care, and pet care,* which includes time spent gardening, doing yard work, playing with one's pet, grooming the pet, and walking the pet. Child care and gardening, lawn care, and pet care may conceptually be thought of as nonmarket work, but at least some tasks in these categories (for example, playing with one's child or gardening) may be viewed as leisure activities. By treating these as separate categories, we avoid having to take a stand on whether these categories are leisure or home production activities.

As argued in the introduction, it is possible to define "leisure" as something that is in part characterized by how substitutable time and expenditure on goods are in the production of consumption goods (recall the examples of producing a meal versus producing television viewing). Activities that directly yield utility are obvious candidates for designation as leisure. Our measure of leisure time therefore sums together time spent watching television, socializing (relaxing with friends and family, playing games with friends and family, talking on the telephone, attending or hosting social events, etc.), time spent exercising or participating in sports (playing sports, attending sporting events, running, etc.), reading (reading books and magazines, reading personal mail, reading personal e-mail, etc.), enjoying entertainment events and hobbies (going to the movies or theater, listening to music, using a computer for leisure, doing arts and crafts, playing a musical instrument, etc.), and all other similar activities. We also include activities that provide direct utility but may also be viewed as intermediate inputs into formal or informal market work, such as sleeping, eating, and personal care.

Although we exclude medical care, we include such activities as grooming, having sex, sleeping or napping, and eating at home or in restaurants. Excluding these categories from leisure has little effect on our general results.[4] For the key analyses performed in this monograph, we also report detailed subcategories of leisure. This detail allows the reader to see which components of the total leisure measure are driving the results.

The final time use categories are time spent on *one's own education, one's own medical care, care of other adults*, and *civic and religious activities*. All residual time use categories are collected in an *other* category so that all activities performed by an individual during a day are categorized. Table A-1 lists all the time use categories analyzed in this monograph.

The focus of this monograph is on differences in time allocation by people of different educational attainments and employment status. Persons in these groups may differ on other relevant characteristics, such as age, family size, or marital status. As a result, along with "unconditional" (raw) averages of how individuals allocate their time, we also report "conditional" averages that are adjusted for this demographic variation.[5]

Our primary sample omits persons younger than twenty-one and those older than sixty-five, as well as students of any age and early retirees, in order to minimize the role of time allocation decisions with a strong intertemporal component (such as those associated with education and retirement).[6] We also restricted the sample to include only individuals with complete time diary reports and complete information on age, education, employment status, and family composition. These restrictions, and their resulting impact on the size of our sample, are discussed in the data appendix. In all, our samples include 1,854, 3,115, and 34,697 individuals from, respectively, the 1965, 1985, and 2003–2005 samples.

2

Trends in the Allocation of Time

In this chapter we describe the principal trends in the allocation of time between work and leisure in the United States over the forty years between 1965 and 2005, a period that witnessed dramatic shifts in how individuals allocate their time.

Trends in Average Time Allocation

Table 2-1 summarizes the key demographically adjusted trends. The most obvious change is observed in market work. According to time diaries, in 2003–2005 the average man worked 39.5 hours per week, which, again, includes commuting time. The average for men in 1985 was 43.5 hours per week, and the average in 1965 was 51.2 hours per week.[7] Whereas men thus experienced a decline in market work of nearly 12 hours per week from 1965 to 2003–2005, women recorded an increase of 3.4 hours per week over that period: women in 2003–2005 worked 25.5 hours per week, as opposed to 23.4 hours per week in 1985 and 22.1 hours per week in 1965.

For understandable reasons, relative to other categories, time spent in market work has received the lion's share of attention. Standard household surveys such as the CPS typically restrict time allocation questions to hours spent in market work. As a result, nonmarket time is frequently lumped together into a catch-all "leisure" measure. To the extent that nonmarket (home) production is important and changing over time, changes in leisure time will be poorly explained by changes in time spent away from market work. Detailed time diaries allow us to better describe what activities are taking place in the broad category of nonmarket time. For example,

TABLE 2-1

TIME ALLOCATION BY BROAD TIME USE CATEGORY
AND CHANGES OVER TIME, FULL SAMPLE
(DEMOGRAPHICALLY ADJUSTED), 1965 TO 2003–2005

Hours per week

Time use category	1965	1985	2003–2005
All			
Total market work	35.5	32.6	31.9
Total nonmarket work	22.5	21.2	18.5
Child care	3.9	3.4	5.7
Leisure	101.7	107.1	105.6
Sample size	1,854	3,115	34,697
Men			
Total market work	51.2	43.5	39.5
Total nonmarket work	9.8	14.1	13.3
Child care	1.6	1.6	3.4
Leisure	101.5	105.8	106.2
Sample size	833	1,382	15,344
Women			
Total market work	22.1	23.4	25.5
Total nonmarket work	33.3	27.2	22.9
Child care	5.9	5.1	7.7
Leisure	101.8	108.2	105.1
Sample size	1,021	1,733	19,353

SOURCE: Authors' calculations from data in the Americans' Use of Time surveys and the American Time Use Surveys.

the 3.4-hour-a-week increase in market work for women was accompanied by a decline of 10.4 hours per week in the nonmarket production activities of housework and shopping, while men increased their nonmarket production by 3.5 hours per week. Both men and women increased time spent on child care by nearly 2 hours per week. These shifts clearly indicate that market work provides an incomplete measure of trends in "total" work, or the sum of time spent in market work and in nonmarket production.

Change, 1965–2005	Change, 1965–1985	Change, 1985–2005
-3.6	-2.9	-0.7
-4.0	-1.3	-2.7
1.8	-0.5	2.2
3.9	5.4	-1.5
-11.7	-7.7	-4.0
3.5	4.3	-0.8
1.8	0.0	1.8
4.7	4.3	0.4
3.4	1.2	2.1
-10.4	-6.1	-4.3
1.8	-0.8	2.6
3.3	6.4	-3.1

NOTE: Examples of activities included in each time use category are listed in table A-1. See the data appendix for a description of the 1965, 1985, and 2003–2005 time use surveys. All averages are calculated using fixed demographic weights to adjust for changing demographics over time, as described in chapter 1. The sample includes all nonstudent, nonretired individuals aged twenty-one to sixty-five (inclusive) who had complete time use reports.

Given the facts just described, it is not surprising that leisure time was able to increase dramatically for both men and women over the last four decades. Men enjoyed a roughly 5-hour-per-week gain in leisure, and women a roughly 3-hour gain, from 1965 to 2003–2005. For both sexes combined, average time spent on leisure in 1965 was 102 hours per week, increasing to 107 hours per week

TABLE 2-2

LEISURE TIME IN THE FULL SAMPLE AND CHANGES
OVER TIME (DEMOGRAPHICALLY ADJUSTED)
BY EDUCATIONAL ATTAINMENT, 1965 TO 2003–2005

Hours per week

Years of schooling	1965	1985	2003–2005
Men			
<12	104.3	104.9	113.0
12	101.2	107.3	107.9
13–15	98.6	104.1	104.4
≥16	101.9	105.8	99.7
Women			
<12	105.7	113.2	111.0
12	101.2	108.4	106.0
13–15	101.0	105.8	102.8
≥16	100.4	105.5	100.2

SOURCE: Authors' calculations from data in the Americans' Use of Time surveys and the American Time Use Surveys.

by 1985 before declining slightly to 106 hours per week in the early 2000s. This broad measure of leisure includes sleeping, eating, and personal care time. Even if we exclude those categories from our measure of leisure, leisure time for the average working-age American increased by 4.6 hours per week between 1965 and 2005.

Trends in Time Allocation by Educational Attainment

One must be careful when considering averages because, as we saw in the differences between the gains for men and women, gains in leisure may not be shared uniformly across the population. In fact, the changes in leisure observed in recent decades differ markedly by educational attainment.

Table 2-2 breaks down the changes in time allocated to leisure between 1965 and 2003–2005 by both sex and educational attainment. One thing that is striking is the similarity of time allocation

Change, 1965–2005	Change, 1965–1985	Change, 1985–2005
8.7	0.5	8.1
6.7	6.1	0.6
5.8	5.5	0.3
−2.2	3.9	−6.1
5.3	7.5	−2.2
4.8	7.2	−2.4
1.8	4.8	−3.0
−0.2	5.1	−5.3

NOTE: The fraction of the sample in each education category is reported in table A-2. The sample includes all nonstudent, nonretired individuals aged twenty-one to sixty-five (inclusive) who had complete time use reports. Averages are calculated using fixed demographic weights to adjust for changing demographics over time, as described in chapter 1.

across educational attainment in 1965. For example, in that year, men with at least sixteen years of schooling spent virtually the same amount of time in leisure (101.9 hours per week) as did men with exactly twelve years of schooling (101.2 hours per week). Men with less than a high school diploma took only 2.4 hours per week more of leisure than college-educated men. By 2003–2005, however, a substantial difference in leisure by educational attainment had emerged. Men with at least sixteen years of schooling now spent less than 100 hours per week in leisure, while men with exactly twelve years of schooling and those with less than twelve years spent, respectively, 108 and 113 hours per week. In other words, on average, leisure for college-educated men declined slightly between 1965 and 2003–2005, while that for men with less education rose sharply. Thus, all of the increase in leisure for the "average" man in table 2-1 is driven by the increase among men with less than a college degree.

Moreover, even though, as shown above, almost all of the increase in leisure for the whole population occurred between 1965 and 1985, the divergence in leisure by educational attainment started after 1985. In 1985 both college-educated men and high school–educated men allocated roughly the same amount of time to leisure (105.8 versus 107.3 hours per week). The timing of the change in inequality in leisure across education groups thus mirrors the well-documented timing of the change in inequality in wages and consumption (see Katz and Autor 1999 and Attanasio, Battistin, and Ichimura 2004 for wages and consumption, respectively).

The pattern is similar for women, save for when the divergence begins. As with men, the increase in leisure between 1965 and 2003–2005 for women with only a high school diploma (4.8 hours per week) was much larger than the change in leisure for college-educated women (–0.2 hour per week). However, unlike with men, roughly half of the increase in inequality in leisure between women with high educational attainment and those with low educational attainment occurred before 1985. In other words, the dispersion in additional leisure between more- and less-educated women after 1985 is less dramatic than that between more- and less-educated men after 1985.

One major concern with dividing our sample by educational attainment centers on the fact that a larger fraction of men have attended college today than did in the 1980s. In our 1985 sample, 45 percent of the men had at least some college education. In the 2003–2005 sample, that fraction had increased to 56 percent. Therefore, these education groups represent different segments of the population in 1985 than in 2003–2005, and this change could explain why the differences in leisure across educational attainment have grown.

Two facts, however, mitigate this concern. The first is that the dispersion in leisure has occurred throughout the entire leisure distribution, and is not simply an artifact of self-selection out of the less-educated category and into the more-educated category. This result is shown in figures 2-1A and 2-1B, which plot the distribution of time allocated to leisure for men and women in 1985 and 2003–2005.[8] For men, the 2003–2005 leisure distribution is flatter in the middle and has fatter tails (save for the extreme right tail) than

FIGURE 2-1A
DISTRIBUTION OF LEISURE BY SEX—MEN

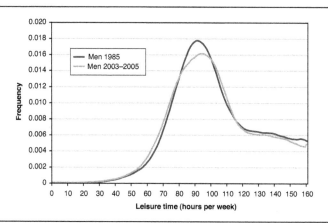

SOURCE: Authors' calculations from data in the Americans' Use of Time surveys and the American Time Use Surveys.
NOTE: Each line depicts a smoothed, continuous estimate (kernel estimate) of the probability density over leisure time in the indicated sample.

FIGURE 2-1B
DISTRIBUTION OF LEISURE BY SEX—WOMEN

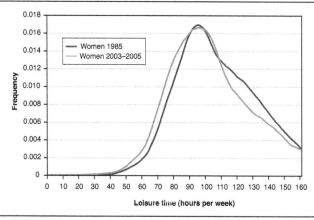

SOURCE: Authors' calculations from data in the Americans' Use of Time surveys and the American Time Use Surveys.
NOTE: Each line depicts a smoothed, continuous estimate (kernel estimate) of the probability density over leisure time in the indicated sample.

the 1985 distribution, indicating a general fanning out of the leisure distribution. As noted above, the spreading out of leisure for women was not as concentrated in the 1985–2005 period as it was for men. This is reflected in figure 2-1B, which shows that although the 2003–2005 leisure distribution is somewhat flatter at the peak than in 1985, the effect is not as dramatic as that for men. Additionally, as we have shown in previous work (figure IV of Aguiar and Hurst 2007a), the increasing dispersion in leisure has occurred at nearly every percentile of the leisure distribution.

The second fact that mitigates the concern about self-selection is that we can identify categories of educational attainment that include similar fractions of the population in each sample. Specifically, roughly 30 percent of men in both 1985 and 2003–2005 had a college diploma or better, and about 13 percent of men in 1985 and 12 percent in 2003–2005 had not finished high school (see table A-2). These two categories thus represent fairly stable fractions of the population. Even so, table 2-2 indicates that the average amount of leisure taken by individuals in these two educational categories diverges after 1985.

Over all, the results described above show that leisure has increased dramatically, on average, since 1965. Most of the increase for the average household occurred before 1985. After 1985, more-educated individuals experienced a leisure reversal while less-educated individuals continued their leisure gains.

3

Time Allocation by Educational Attainment and Employment Status

The trends presented in the previous chapter raise interesting questions regarding what has driven the growing "leisure gap" among groups with different levels of educational attainment. One natural question is whether the relative gains in leisure for less-educated men reflect increases in involuntary unemployment or disability. More generally, how much of the increase in leisure dispersion across education groups reflects differences in the relative incidence of unemployment or disability across those groups? Shedding light on such questions is the focus of this chapter. We confine our analysis to men, given that less-educated men experienced the sharpest decline in market work and therefore the issue of involuntary leisure due to employment status may be particularly relevant for them.[9]

We concentrate on trends between 1985 and 2003–2005 because, as already noted, this period witnessed the dramatic increase in leisure differences across educational attainment for men. We begin by documenting that trends in employment status over this period vary markedly by education category, with less-educated men experiencing larger declines in employment.[10] We then explore in detail the differences in time allocation both within and between employment status categories for the 1985 and the 2003–2005 periods. This analysis will allow us to identify and further explore the extent to which leisure differences can be attributed to differences in the rate of employment, the topic that is the focus of chapter 4.

TABLE 3-1
EMPLOYMENT STATUS OF MEN BY EDUCATIONAL ATTAINMENT,
1985 AND 2003–2005

Employment status	All men	Less-educated men
1985		
Share employed	91%	89%
Share nonemployed	9%	11%
Unemployed	3%	4%
Other nonemployed	6%	7%
2003–2005		
Share employed	88%	83%
Share nonemployed	12%	17%
Unemployed	4%	5%
Disabled	5%	8%
Other nonemployed	3%	4%

SOURCE: Authors' calculations from data in the Americans' Use of Time surveys and the American Time Use Surveys.

Employment Status by Educational Attainment

Table 3-1 documents employment patterns by level of education in 1985 and 2003–2005. Unlike the numbers in the previous chapter, these data on employment patterns are unconditional on demographics. That is, they have not been adjusted for changes in the age distribution of the population or the changing family composition that occurred during the past twenty years. However, differences in the allocation of time between education groups conditional on demographic differences are also shown in all subsequent tables. For the remainder of our analysis, we focus on only two education categories: more educated (those with more than twelve years of schooling) and less educated (those with twelve years or less of schooling). This classification is dictated by the relatively small sample in the 1985 survey. For example, the 1985 sample includes only fifteen nonemployed men who were college graduates.

More-educated men	Demographically adjusted difference (percentage points)
94%	–4
6%	4
2%	2
4%	2
92%	–9
8%	9
4%	2
2%	5
3%	2

NOTE: Sample is the same as the subsample "men" in tables 2-1 and 2-2. Less-educated men are those with twelve years of education or less, and more-educated men are those with more than twelve years of education. All averages in columns 1–3 are unconditional on demographic characteristics. Column 4 reports the difference between column 2 and column 3, adjusted for demographic differences across education categories as described in chapter 1 of the text. See the text for a discussion of the employment status categories.

The top panel of table 3-1 shows employment patterns by educational attainment for men in 1985. The first line reports that 89 percent (column 2) of men with a high school diploma or less were employed, whereas 94 percent (column 3) of men with more than twelve years of education were employed. Adjusting for differences in demographics between the two groups, we find a 4-percentage-point difference in the probability of being employed between more- and less-educated men.

The bottom panel of table 3-1 reports the same statistics for 2003–2005. By this period the average employment rate had fallen slightly, from 91 percent to 88 percent. However, the decline is much larger among less-educated men, from 89 percent in 1985 to 83 percent in 2003–2005. More-educated men saw a smaller decline, from 94 percent to 92 percent. This relative decline in employment among less-educated men generated an employment gap of 9 percentage points in 2003–2005.

In the 1985 survey we can distinguish unemployed from other nonemployed individuals. (As discussed above, we have excluded students and retirees from our analysis.) Making this distinction reveals that most of the relatively small gap in employment rates in 1985 reflects both a higher unemployment rate and a higher rate of other nonemployment among the less educated than among the more educated. We can achieve a finer breakdown of the nonemployed in 2003–2005.[11] The bottom panel of table 3-1 reports that the employment gap between less- and more-educated men results from educational differences in all other job status categories that favor the more educated. For example, conditional on demographics, less-educated men were 5 percentage points more likely to be disabled. The sharp rise in disability over the last twenty years has been well documented in the literature (see, for example, Autor and Duggan 2003). Although disability status was not part of the 1985 survey, the small rates of "other" nonemployed in 1985 and the large gap observed in 2003–2005 suggest that disability rates increased disproportionately among the less educated.

Time Allocation in 1985 by Employment Status

We now turn to the important question of whether these trends in employment status are the driving force behind the differential increase in leisure for the less educated. Tables 3-2A, 3-2B, and 3-2C report time spent on key activities in 1985 broken down by educational attainment and employment status. We show a broad set of time use categories, including subcategories for leisure, to provide a detailed picture of how individuals are allocating their time.[12] We use the same categories in tables 3-3A, 3-3B, 3-3C, 3-4A, 3-4B, and 3-4C for the 2003–2005 data.

Table 3-2A averages overall employment groups, while table 3-2B narrows the focus to employed men and table 3-2C restricts the sample to nonemployed men, a group that includes the unemployed, the disabled, and others out of the labor force. Table 3-2A indicates that time allocation is similar for a number of activities between less- and more-educated men. For example, less-educated men performed 0.3 hour per week less market labor and 1.4 hours per week less home production (demographically adjusted) than their more-educated counterparts. The net effect is that in 1985 the less educated enjoyed 1.6 hours per week more leisure than the more educated. These results are consistent with those reported in table 2-2, which showed that in 1985 there was little difference in leisure across education groups. The similarity of time allocation patterns within broad categories between education groups does mask some sharp differences in time allocated to activities within those categories. For example, less-educated men watched seventeen hours per week of television, compared with thirteen hours per week for more-educated men. This difference is offset by the less-educated men reading and sleeping less than their more-educated counterparts.

Conditional on employment (table 3-2B) and adjusting for demographic differences (column 5), in 1985 less-educated men performed 1.4 hours per week more market work and 1.3 hours per week less nonmarket work than their more-educated counterparts. Interestingly, conditional on employment, there is essentially no difference in leisure at all (0.2 hour per week) across education groups in 1985. The educational differences in table 3-2B for employed workers are consistent with the overall averages in table 3-2A, including the relative differences in television watching, sleeping, and reading.

The time use diaries also collect data on informal market work as defined in chapter 1. This type of work may be important for those who are officially nonemployed. Time use diaries also collect data on job search, which includes activities such as contacting potential employers, sending out resumes, researching details about jobs, submitting applications, searching for open jobs (reading the classifieds, using Internet job search websites), interviewing for jobs (in person or over the phone), preparing for job interviews, and traveling to interviews. A third market-related activity is education and training, which includes time spent in formal degree programs (time in the classroom plus time spent on homework and the associated

TABLE 3-2A

TIME ALLOCATION BY DETAILED TIME USE CATEGORY
AND EDUCATIONAL ATTAINMENT FOR ALL MEN, 1985
Hours per week

Time use category	All	Less-educated
Total market work (exc. job search)	43.0	42.5
Job search	0.1	0.3
Education and training	0.7	0.5
Total nonmarket work	13.0	12.5
Home and vehicle maintenance	3.0	3.6
Obtaining goods and services	4.7	4.2
All other home production	1.5	1.1
Child care	1.6	1.5
Gardening, lawn care, pet care	0.7	0.7
Total leisure	106.4	107.4
Television watching	15.1	17.1
Socializing	7.6	8.1
Exercise and sport	3.1	2.9
Reading	3.1	2.1
Hobbies and other entertainment	1.7	1.6
Eating	8.0	8.1
Sleeping	54.9	54.6
Personal care	8.7	8.7
Own medical care	0.2	0.2
Care of other adults	0.5	0.7
Religious and civic activities	1.7	1.8
Other	NA	NA
Sample size	1,382	761

SOURCE: Authors' calculations from data in the Americans' Use of Time surveys and the American Time Use Surveys.
NOTES: Less-educated men are those with twelve years of education or less, and more-educated men are those with more than twelve years of education. Means in columns 1–4 are unconditional on demographic characteristics. Differences in the final column are adjusted for

More-educated	Unconditional difference	Demographically adjusted difference
43.8	−1.3	−0.3
0.0	0.2	0.3
0.9	−0.4	−0.3
13.6	−1.2	−1.4
2.3	1.3	1.2
5.2	−1.0	−1.0
1.9	−0.8	−0.9
1.8	−0.3	−0.1
0.8	−0.1	−0.3
105.1	2.2	1.6
12.6	4.5	4.7
6.9	1.2	0.9
3.2	−0.3	−0.2
4.4	−2.3	−2.5
1.8	−0.3	−0.3
8.0	0.1	−0.1
55.1	−0.5	−0.8
8.6	0.1	0.1
0.3	−0.1	−0.1
0.2	0.5	0.4
1.5	0.3	0.3
NA	NA	NA
621		

demographic differences across education categories as described in chapter 1. The sample includes all nonstudent, nonretired men aged twenty-one to sixty-five (inclusive) who had complete time use reports. Examples of activities included in each time use category are listed in table A-1. NA = not available.

TABLE 3-2B

TIME ALLOCATION BY DETAILED TIME USE CATEGORY
AND EDUCATIONAL ATTAINMENT FOR EMPLOYED MEN, 1985
Hours per week

Time use category	All	Less-educated
Total market work (exc. job search)	47.1	47.5
Job search	0.0	0.0
Education and training	0.7	0.5
Total nonmarket work	11.9	11.4
Home and vehicle maintenance	2.8	3.4
Obtaining goods and services	4.4	3.9
All other home production	1.4	1.1
Child care	1.6	1.6
Gardening, lawn care, pet care	0.7	0.7
Total leisure	103.7	103.9
Television watching	14.2	15.8
Socializing	7.1	7.4
Exercise and sport	2.9	2.8
Reading	3.0	2.0
Hobbies and other entertainment	1.6	1.4
Eating	7.9	7.9
Sleeping	54.2	53.9
Personal care	8.7	8.7
Own medical care	0.2	0.1
Care of other adults	0.4	0.6
Religious and civic activities	1.6	1.7
Other	NA	NA
Sample size	1,258	675

SOURCE: Authors' calculations from data in the Americans' Use of Time surveys and the American Time Use Surveys.
NOTES: Less-educated men are those with twelve years of education or less, and more-educated men are those with more than twelve years of education. Means in columns 1–4 are unconditional on demographic characteristics. Differences in the final column are adjusted for

More-educated	Unconditional difference	Demographically adjusted difference
46.6	1.0	1.4
0.0	0.0	0.0
1.0	-0.5	-0.4
12.6	-1.2	-1.3
2.0	1.4	1.2
4.9	-1.0	-1.0
1.8	-0.7	-0.7
1.6	-0.1	0.1
0.8	-0.1	-0.3
103.5	0.5	0.2
12.4	3.4	3.5
6.7	0.7	0.5
3.1	-0.3	-0.1
4.2	-2.2	-2.3
1.7	-0.2	-0.2
7.8	0.0	0.0
54.6	-0.6	-1.1
8.8	-0.1	0.0
0.2	-0.1	-0.1
0.2	0.5	0.4
1.5	0.2	0.2
NA	NA	NA
583		

demographic differences across education categories as described in chapter 1. The sample includes all nonstudent, nonretired men aged twenty-one to sixty five (inclusive) who had complete time use reports. Examples of activities included in each time use category are listed in table A-1. NA = not available.

TABLE 3-2C
TIME ALLOCATION BY DETAILED TIME USE CATEGORY AND
EDUCATIONAL ATTAINMENT FOR NONEMPLOYED MEN, 1985
Hours per week

Time use category	All	Less-educated
Total market work (exc. job search)	2.2	2.4
Job search	1.5	2.2
Education and training	0.6	0.9
Total nonmarket work	23.7	21.3
Home and vehicle maintenance	5.6	5.3
Obtaining goods and services	7.3	6.3
All other home production	2.1	1.1
Child care	2.1	1.1
Gardening, lawn care, pet care	0.8	1.0
Total leisure	133.2	134.6
Television watching	24.0	27.7
Socializing	12.6	13.6
Exercise and sport	4.3	3.7
Reading	4.7	3.1
Hobbies and other entertainment	3.1	2.5
Eating	9.6	9.5
Sleeping	61.3	60.4
Personal care	8.2	8.9
Own medical care	0.9	0.9
Care of other adults	0.9	1.1
Religious and civic activities	2.1	2.6
Other	NA	NA
Sample size	124	86

SOURCE: Authors' calculations from data in the Americans' Use of Time surveys and the American Time Use Surveys.
NOTES: Less-educated men are those with twelve years of education or less, and more-educated men are those with more than twelve years of education. Means in columns 1–4 are unconditional on demographic characteristics. Differences in the final column are adjusted for

More-educated	Unconditional difference	Demographically adjusted difference
1.9	0.5	1.0
0.2	2.0	2.5
0.1	0.8	0.6
29.0	−7.7	−5.3
6.3	−1.0	−1.6
9.4	−3.1	−1.7
4.4	−3.3	−2.0
4.2	−3.1	−1.8
0.4	0.6	0.4
130.0	4.6	1.3
15.8	11.9	11.8
10.4	3.2	0.3
5.6	−1.9	−2.3
8.2	−5.1	−4.7
4.3	−1.8	−0.9
10.0	−0.5	−0.9
63.4	−3.0	−2.6
6.6	2.3	2.0
0.7	0.2	0.1
0.6	0.5	0.3
1.0	1.6	1.0
NA	NA	NA
38		

demographic differences across education categories as described in chapter 1. The sample includes all nonstudent, nonretired men aged twenty-one to sixty-five (inclusive) who had complete time use reports. Examples of activities included in each time use category are listed in table A-1. NA = not available.

commuting time) as well as professional exam preparation (e.g., preparing to get a real estate license or studying for the bar exam) and nondegree course work (e.g., taking a financial planning class or a cooking class).

Table 3-2C indicates that when out of work, less-educated men in 1985 performed more informal market work and engaged in more searching for new employment and in more education and training than did their more-educated counterparts. However, the less-educated nonemployed men performed less nonmarket work and child care. The net effect is that the less-educated nonemployed men enjoyed roughly 1 hour more of leisure per week than did more-educated non-employed men. The less-educated men spent more of their leisure time watching television and socializing than reading or exercising.

Overall, tables 3-2A, 3-2B, and 3-2C indicate a striking similar-ity in the allocation of time across educational attainment in 1985. Time allocation to key aggregates (e.g., market work, home pro-duction, and leisure) does not differ markedly between less- and more-educated men. Moreover, rates of employment are similar across education groups. These patterns combine to generate little difference in average leisure between less- and more-educated men.

A comparison of tables 3-2B and 3-2C reveals that nonemployed men in 1985 on average enjoyed nearly thirty hours more per week in leisure than their employed counterparts, while performing only about twelve hours more per week of nonmarket production and child care. Almost all elements of leisure show an increase when men move from employed to nonemployed status, with the biggest gains coming in the television watching and sleeping categories. The fact that nonemployed men enjoyed more leisure than employed men in 1985 suggests that the differences in employment rates observed in 2003–2005 may be an important factor in explaining the recent leisure gap, a possibility we explore next.

Time Allocation in 2003–2005 by Employment Status

Tables 3-3A, 3-3B, and 3-3C repeat the analysis of tables 3-2A, 3-2B, and 3-2C using the 2003–2005 sample of men. Table 3-3A reports education group averages for all men without considering their employment status. In contrast to the patterns seen in the 1985 data (and as anticipated by the data patterns in table 2-2), there are significant differences in time use across education groups in the 2003–2005 data. In particular, less-educated men experienced 7.1 hours per week more leisure than men with more education. Less-educated men were able to have these additional hours because they allocated 4.6 hours per week less to market work, 0.7 hour less to nonmarket work, 0.7 hour per week less to child care, and 1.1 hours less to education and training.

Tables 3-3B and 3-3C report the allocation of time for employed and nonemployed men, respectively. As noted above, the ATUS survey allows us to break out the unemployed and disabled separately. However, we initially consider these two groups together so that we can compare all nonemployed men in 2003–2005 with nonemployed men in 1985. We examine the patterns for the various subcategories of nonemployed men in tables 3-4A, 3-4B, and 3-4C.

Conditional on working, and adjusting for demographic differences, more-educated men engaged in market work one hour per week more than less-educated men. Despite the similarity in the number of hours worked by employed men regardless of their educational attainment, more-educated men spent four hours per week less in leisure. To put this in perspective, over the course of a year, less-educated employed men experienced an average of 7.6 full (twenty-four-hour) days more leisure than more-educated men. This is equivalent to roughly 4.5 additional forty-hour weeks of vacation time for less-educated employed men relative to their more-educated counterparts.

The fact that less-educated employed men reported one hour less per week of market work but enjoyed four hours per week more of leisure raises the question of where this additional leisure time came from. The answer is that less-educated employed men spent less time doing activities in nearly every category other than market work. They spent one hour per week less on nonmarket work, one hour less on child care, one hour less on education and training, and half an hour less on religious and civic activities than more-educated

TABLE 3-3A
TIME ALLOCATION BY DETAILED TIME USE CATEGORY AND
EDUCATIONAL ATTAINMENT FOR ALL MEN, 2003–2005
Hours per week

Time use category	All	Less-educated
Total market work (exc. job search)	39.7	36.9
Job search	0.2	0.2
Education and training	0.9	0.4
Total nonmarket work	11.3	10.9
Home and vehicle maintenance	2.5	2.7
Obtaining goods and services	4.2	3.9
All other home production	1.1	0.9
Child care	3.1	2.7
Gardening, lawn care, pet care	2.1	2.2
Total leisure	105.6	109.8
Television watching	18.1	21.6
Socializing	6.8	7.1
Exercise and sport	2.8	2.6
Reading	1.9	1.2
Hobbies and other entertainment	2.3	1.9
Eating	8.9	8.2
Sleeping	58.1	60.1
Personal care	4.2	4.0
Own medical care	0.8	0.8
Care of other adults	1.5	1.7
Religious and civic activities	1.7	1.5
Other	0.9	0.8
Sample size	15,344	5,831

SOURCE: Authors' calculations from data in the Americans' Use of Time surveys and the American Time Use Surveys.
NOTE: Less-educated men are those with twelve years of education or less, and more-educated men are those with more than twelve years of education. Means in columns 1–4 are

More-educated	Unconditional difference	Demographically adjusted difference
41.9	−5.0	−4.6
0.3	−0.1	−0.1
1.3	−1.0	−1.1
11.7	−0.8	−0.7
2.4	0.4	0.4
4.4	−0.5	−0.5
1.3	−0.4	−0.4
3.4	−0.7	−0.7
2.1	0.1	0.2
102.3	7.5	7.1
15.3	6.3	6.0
6.5	0.6	0.5
3.1	−0.5	−0.5
2.5	−1.3	−1.3
2.7	−0.8	−0.8
9.4	−1.2	−1.2
56.5	3.5	3.3
4.3	−0.3	−0.3
0.7	0.1	0.1
1.4	0.2	0.2
1.9	−0.4	−0.4
0.9	−0.1	−0.1
9,513		

unconditional on demographic characteristics. Differences in the final column are adjusted for demographic differences across education categories as described in chapter 1. The sample includes all nonstudent, nonretired men aged twenty-one to sixty-five (inclusive) who had complete time use reports.

TABLE 3-3B
TIME ALLOCATION BY DETAILED TIME USE CATEGORY AND
EDUCATIONAL ATTAINMENT FOR EMPLOYED MEN, 2003–2005
Hours per week

Time use category	All	Less-educated
Total market work (exc. job search)	45.1	44.5
Job search	0.1	0.1
Education and training	0.9	0.3
Total nonmarket work	10.7	10.0
Home and vehicle maintenance	2.3	2.4
Obtaining goods and services	4.2	3.9
All other home production	1.0	0.8
Child care	3.1	2.6
Gardening, lawn care, pet care	2.0	2.2
Total leisure	101.7	104.1
Television watching	16.0	18.4
Socializing	6.2	6.3
Exercise and sport	2.9	2.5
Reading	1.8	1.0
Hobbies and other entertainment	2.1	1.6
Eating	9.0	8.4
Sleeping	57.1	58.7
Personal care	4.3	4.2
Own medical care	0.6	0.5
Care of other adults	1.5	1.6
Religious and civic activities	1.6	1.3
Other	0.8	0.7
Sample size	13,505	4,793

SOURCE: Authors' calculations from data in the Americans' Use of Time surveys and the American Time Use Surveys.
Note: Less-educated men are those with twelve years of education or less, and more-educated men are those with more than twelve years of education. Means in columns 1–4

More-educated	Unconditional difference	Demographically adjusted difference
45.5	−1.0	−0.9
0.1	0.0	0.0
1.3	−1.0	−1.1
11.1	−1.1	−1.0
2.2	0.2	0.3
4.4	−0.5	−0.5
1.2	−0.3	−0.3
3.4	−0.8	−0.9
1.9	0.3	0.3
100.1	4.1	3.9
14.3	4.1	4.0
6.2	0.1	0.1
3.1	−0.6	−0.6
2.4	−1.3	−1.3
2.5	−0.8	−0.8
9.5	−1.1	−1.1
55.9	2.8	2.6
4.4	−0.2	−0.2
0.6	−0.1	−0.1
1.3	0.3	0.3
1.8	−0.5	−0.5
0.8	−0.1	−0.1
8,712		

are unconditional on demographic characteristics. Differences in the final column are adjusted for demographic differences across education categories as described in chapter 1. The sample includes all nonstudent, nonretired men aged twenty-one to sixty-five (inclusive) who had complete time use reports.

TABLE 3-3C
TIME ALLOCATION BY DETAILED TIME USE CATEGORY AND
EDUCATIONAL ATTAINMENT FOR NONEMPLOYED MEN, 2003–2005
Hours per week

Time use category	All	Less-educated
Total market work (exc. job search)	1.6	1.1
Job search	1.4	0.7
Education and training	0.9	0.5
Total nonmarket work	15.9	14.7
Home and vehicle maintenance	4.0	4.0
Obtaining goods and services	4.6	4.1
All other home production	1.6	1.1
Child care	3.5	3.4
Gardening, lawn care, pet care	3.0	2.4
Total leisure	133.2	137.1
Television watching	32.8	36.7
Socializing	10.5	10.9
Exercise and sport	2.8	2.8
Reading	2.7	1.9
Hobbies and other entertainment	4.0	3.3
Eating	7.9	7.3
Sleeping	65.1	66.4
Personal care	3.3	3.2
Own medical care	2.3	2.4
Care of other adults	2.2	2.0
Religious and civic activities	2.5	2.3
Other	1.5	1.3
Sample size	1,839	1,038

SOURCE: Authors' calculations from data in the Americans' Use of Time surveys and the American Time Use Surveys.
NOTE: Less-educated men are those with twelve years of education or less, and more-educated men are those with more than twelve years of education. Means in columns 1–4 are

More-educated	Unconditional difference	Demographically adjusted difference
2.4	−1.3	−1.2
2.5	−1.8	−1.9
1.6	−1.0	−1.0
17.8	−3.1	−2.7
4.1	−0.1	0.2
5.3	−1.2	−1.1
2.3	−1.2	−1.4
3.7	−0.3	−0.7
3.8	−1.4	−1.4
126.9	10.2	9.7
26.5	10.2	10.0
9.9	1.0	0.8
2.9	−0.1	−0.1
4.1	−2.3	−2.3
5.1	−1.8	−1.8
8.8	−1.4	−1.3
62.9	3.5	3.3
3.5	−0.3	−0.1
2.1	0.3	0.3
2.5	−0.5	−0.6
2.8	−0.4	−0.1
1.8	−0.5	−0.5
801		

unconditional on demographic characteristics. Differences in the final column are adjusted for demographic differences across education categories as described in chapter 1. The sample includes all nonstudent, nonretired men aged twenty-one to sixty-five (inclusive) who had complete time use reports.

employed men. Less-educated employed men did spend slightly more time (about a half hour per week) on gardening and pet care and care of other adults. The education gap within the nonmarket sector for employed men is driven by the fact that more-educated men spent more time on cooking and indoor housecleaning (the primary component of "all other home production") and shopping, whereas less-educated men spent slightly more time on home and vehicle maintenance.

An additional striking fact from table 3-3B is that more than 100 percent of the conditional differences in leisure between educational groups for working men can be attributed to differences in time spent watching television. Working men with a high school diploma or less spent four hours more per week watching television than more-educated working men. Although more-educated men spent more time exercising, reading, and pursuing other hobbies, and less time sleeping and socializing, the net effect of all these other differences in leisure components across education groups is essentially zero.

The results in table 3-3B imply that differences in employment status are not the full story behind the large leisure gap between less- and more-educated men. However, the four-hour-per-week gap between less- and more-educated employed men is much smaller than the 7.1-hour-per-week difference for the full sample. Given that most men within each education group are employed, the remainder of the difference in leisure documented in table 3-3A must come from either differences in job status among education groups or differences in time use within the nonemployed job status categories among education groups.

Table 3-3C indicates that educational differences among nonemployed men are reflected in different time allocation choices. Relative to more-educated nonemployed men, less-educated nonemployed men devote 1.2 hours less to informal market work per week, 1.9 hours less to job search, 1.0 hour less to education and training, 2.7 hours less to nonmarket work, 1.4 hours less to gardening, lawn care, and pet care, 0.6 hour less to care of other adults, and 0.7 hour less to child care. These differences translate into nearly ten hours more per week spent on leisure. Table 3-3C thus indicates that employment status is not the only source of leisure differences between less-educated and more-educated men. Less-educated nonemployed men allocate their time very differently than their more-educated counterparts.

The results from 1985 (table 3-2C) indicate that this was not the case twenty years earlier. The twenty years after 1985 saw a dramatic shift in the time allocation patterns of less-educated nonemployed men. The average nonemployed man with a high school education or less spent 134.6 hours per week in leisure in 1985, but 137.1 hours per week in 2003–2005. Conversely, leisure time declined by over three hours per week for more-educated nonemployed men.

The change over time for less-educated nonemployed men was accompanied by a sharp decline in their home production, job search, and informal market work between 1985 and 2003–2005. In 1985, for example, less-educated nonemployed men spent relatively more time searching for jobs than did more-educated nonemployed men. This pattern reversed in 2003–2005, perhaps reflecting changes in the separate job markets faced by men of different education levels, and changes in the reasons that less-educated men are nonemployed (namely, the rise in the disability rate and the rising rate of "other" nonemployment between 1985 and 2003–2005).

These results suggest that from 1985 to 2003–2005 the allocation of time by less-educated nonemployed men shifted dramatically compared with the changes in time allocation seen for more-educated nonemployed men. In particular, the nature of nonemployment changed for less-educated men in 2003–2005, relative to that for both more-educated and less-educated men in 1985. A key part of this large change is that a less-educated nonemployed man in 2003-2005 was more likely to be disabled than his 1985 counterpart (Autor and Duggan 2003). Disabilities may also explain the drop in other forms of work by the nonemployed. To explore this possibility, in tables 3-4A, 3-4B, and 3-4C, we separately report time allocation in 2003–2005 for unemployed, disabled, and other nonemployed men, respectively.

Table 3-4A indicates that in 2003–2005, unemployed men with a high school diploma or less spent 6.4 more hours per week on

TABLE 3-4A

TIME ALLOCATION BY DETAILED TIME USE CATEGORY AND
EDUCATIONAL ATTAINMENT FOR UNEMPLOYED MEN, 2003–2005
Hours per week

Time use category	All	Less-educated
Total market work (exc. job search)	3.4	3.0
Job search	3.9	2.4
Education and training	1.4	0.9
Total nonmarket work	19.0	18.7
Home and vehicle maintenance	5.9	7.0
Obtaining goods and services	5.2	4.7
All other home production	2.0	1.4
Child care	4.3	4.4
Gardening, lawn care, pet care	3.3	2.3
Total leisure	124.9	127.9
Television watching	26.2	29.7
Socializing	11.8	13.3
Exercise and sport	3.3	3.0
Reading	2.3	1.4
Hobbies and other entertainment	3.7	1.3
Eating	7.8	7.0
Sleeping	62.7	64.7
Personal care	4.0	4.0
Own medical care	0.5	0.6
Care of other adults	2.7	3.0
Religious and civic activities	2.5	2.4
Other	2.1	2.5
Sample size	596	283

SOURCE: Authors' calculations from data in the Americans' Use of Time surveys and the American Time Use Surveys.
NOTE: Less-educated men are those with twelve years of education or less, and more-educated men are those with more than twelve years of education. Means in columns 1–4

More-educated	Unconditional difference	Demographically adjusted difference
3.8	−0.8	−0.5
5.5	−3.2	−2.9
2.1	−1.3	−1.2
19.2	−0.5	−0.1
4.7	2.2	2.4
5.9	−1.2	−1.2
2.7	−1.3	−1.1
4.2	0.2	−0.5
4.5	−2.2	−2.2
121.5	6.4	5.5
22.2	7.6	7.5
10.0	3.4	2.7
3.5	−0.5	−0.5
3.4	−2.0	−1.9
6.4	−5.1	−5.0
8.7	−1.8	−1.4
60.5	4.2	3.4
4.1	−0.1	−0.3
0.5	0.1	0.2
2.4	0.6	0.8
2.6	−0.2	0.1
1.6	0.9	0.8
313		

are unconditional on demographic characteristics. Differences in the final column are adjusted for demographic differences across education categories as described in chapter 1. The sample includes all nonstudent, nonretired men aged twenty-one to sixty-five (inclusive) who had complete time use reports.

leisure than did more-educated unemployed men. The difference falls to 5.5 hours per week after controlling for demographic differences, such as age and family size, across the education groups. As with their employed counterparts, the increase in leisure for less-educated unemployed men in 2003–2005 is driven by the fact that they watched more television (an additional 7.5 hours per week), socialized more (2.7 hours per week), and slept more (3.4 hours per week) than more-educated unemployed men. That less-educated unemployed men spent less time reading (1.9 hours per week), eating (1.4 hours per week), exercising and participating in sports (0.5 hour per week), and engaging in hobbies and other entertainment (5.0 hours per week) than more-educated unemployed men also factors into the leisure gap we observe between the two groups.

Where does the increase in leisure for less-educated unemployed men in this period come from? A striking fact is that these men spent 2.9 hours less per week searching for employment than did their more-educated counterparts. This difference alone can account for nearly 53 percent of the conditional difference in leisure between less- and more-educated unemployed men. However, this finding may understate the true amount of job search going on. For example, when unemployed men (whether less or more educated) "socialize," they may also be networking or inquiring about potential job leads.

How did more-educated unemployed men spend their leisure time in 2003–2005? They spent roughly 5.5 hours per week on job search and 2.1 hours per week on education and training. Taken together, more-educated unemployed men spent 4.1 hours per week more than less-educated unemployed men increasing their future job prospects by either looking for a new job or increasing their human capital. More-educated unemployed men also spent 0.5 hour per week more than did less-educated men working for pay in the informal sector. These differences in time spent on job search, education, and work for pay in the informal sector account for nearly 84 percent of the difference in leisure between more- and less-educated unemployed men in this period.

The total time spent on nonmarket work in 2003–2005 is similar between more- and less-educated unemployed men, although the types of nonmarket work these groups engaged in differ. More-educated unemployed men spent more time shopping, preparing meals, and cleaning the home (the latter two are the primary components of "all other home production"), and less time on home and vehicle maintenance. Less-educated unemployed men spent 0.5 hour less per week on child care (conditional on demographics) and 2.2 hours less per week on gardening, lawn care, and pet care.

In table 3-4B, we focus on men who are not employed because they are disabled. As we saw in table 3-1, disability rates differ markedly by educational attainment and are therefore a potentially important source of time allocation differences. The data show that the unconditional leisure gap across educational levels is 5.4 hours per week for disabled men, similar to that between less- and more-educated employed men (4.1 hours per week) and less- and more-educated unemployed men (6.4 hours per week). Adjusting for demographics, the leisure gap between less- and more-educated disabled men is 5.7 hours per week.

The fact that educational differences in leisure are similar among employed and unemployed men masks the fact that disabled men spent significantly more time in leisure than their unemployed or their employed counterparts. Less-educated disabled men spent 144 hours per week in leisure in 2003–2005, compared with 104 hours for less-educated employed men and 128 hours per week for less-educated unemployed men. Note that the forty-hour-per-week difference in leisure between less-educated employed men and less-educated disabled men is similar to the forty-five hours per week that less-educated employed men spent in market work. The remaining five hours are mostly accounted for by medical care. That is, very little of disabled men's time not allocated to market work was reallocated to nonmarket work or child care. A similar pattern holds for more-educated disabled men as well.

The additional leisure enjoyed by less-educated disabled men relative to more-educated disabled men was used primarily in three activities: nonmarket production (2.2 hours per week), education (1.4 hours per week), and care of other adults (1.3 hours per week).

TABLE 3-4B

TIME ALLOCATION BY DETAILED TIME USE CATEGORY AND
EDUCATIONAL ATTAINMENT FOR DISABLED MEN, 2003–2005

Hours per week

Time use category	All	Less-educated
Total market work (exc. job search)	0.2	0.0
Job search	0.0	0.0
Education and training	0.6	0.2
Total nonmarket work	11.1	10.6
Home and vehicle maintenance	1.8	2.0
Obtaining goods and services	3.1	2.9
All other home production	0.8	0.6
Child care	2.4	2.5
Gardening, lawn care, pet care	2.0	2.2
Total leisure	142.7	144.1
Television watching	41.4	43.2
Socializing	9.7	9.8
Exercise and sport	2.0	2.3
Reading	3.2	2.6
Hobbies and other entertainment	4.2	4.1
Eating	7.4	7.4
Sleeping	67.2	67.2
Personal care	2.9	2.8
Own medical care	4.3	4.2
Care of other adults	1.5	1.2
Religious and civic activities	2.2	2.2
Other	1.0	0.8
Sample size	758	521

SOURCE: Authors' calculations from data in the Americans' Use of Time surveys and the American Time Use Surveys.

NOTE: Less-educated men are those with twelve years of education or less, and more-educated men are those with more than twelve years of education. Means in columns 1–4

More-educated	Unconditional difference	Demographically adjusted difference
0.7	-0.7	-0.7
0.2	-0.2	-0.2
1.6	-1.4	-1.7
12.8	-2.2	-1.8
1.3	0.8	0.9
3.9	-1.0	-0.8
1.6	-1.0	-1.3
2.0	0.4	0.2
1.3	0.9	1.0
138.7	5.4	5.7
36.0	7.3	7.5
9.2	0.6	0.4
1.1	1.2	1.2
4.8	-2.2	-2.0
4.4	-0.4	-0.2
7.6	-0.2	-0.2
67.2	0.0	-0.2
2.9	-0.1	0.0
4.6	-0.4	-0.5
2.5	-1.3	-1.4
2.1	0.1	0.1
1.5	-0.7	-0.8
237		

are unconditional on demographic characteristics. Differences in the final column are adjusted for demographic differences across education categories as described in chapter 1. The sample includes all nonstudent, nonretired men aged twenty-one to sixty-five (inclusive) who had complete time use reports.

TABLE 3-4C

TIME ALLOCATION BY DETAILED TIME USE CATEGORY AND
EDUCATIONAL ATTAINMENT FOR OTHER NON-EMPLOYED MEN,
2003–2005

Hours per week

Time use category	All	Less-educated
Total market work (exc. job search)	1.3	0.8
Job search	0.2	0.0
Education and training	0.8	0.8
Total nonmarket work	18.7	17.5
Home and vehicle maintenance	4.7	4.0
Obtaining goods and services	5.8	5.8
All other home production	2.0	1.7
Child care	4.2	4.0
Gardening, lawn care, pet care	3.9	3.0
Total leisure	130.5	135.2
Television watching	29.3	32.9
Socializing	10.2	10.1
Exercise and sport	3.4	3.4
Reading	2.6	1.0
Hobbies and other entertainment	4.0	4.2
Eating	8.6	7.7
Sleeping	65.1	67.0
Personal care	3.0	2.9
Own medical care	1.8	1.4
Care of other adults	2.3	2.2
Religious and civic activities	3.0	2.5
Other	1.3	0.6
Sample size	485	234

SOURCE: Authors' calculations from data in the Americans' Use of Time surveys and the American Time Use Surveys.

NOTE: Less-educated men are those with twelve years of education or less, and more-educated men are those with more than twelve years of education. Means in columns 1–4 are

More-educated	Unconditional difference	Demographically adjusted difference
2.0	−1.2	−1.0
0.3	−0.3	−0.3
0.9	−0.1	−0.1
20.1	−2.6	−3.4
5.5	−1.5	−1.9
5.8	−0.1	−0.2
2.3	−0.6	−0.6
4.5	−0.5	−0.4
5.0	−2.0	−1.4
124.6	10.6	9.8
24.6	8.3	8.5
10.4	−0.3	−0.6
3.5	−0.1	0.2
4.5	−3.5	−3.4
3.8	0.5	0.4
9.7	−2.1	−2.1
62.6	4.4	2.6
3.0	−0.1	−0.2
2.3	−1.0	−1.0
2.5	−0.3	0.0
3.6	−1.0	−0.8
2.2	−1.6	−1.5
251		

unconditional on demographic characteristics. Differences in the final column are adjusted for demographic differences across education categories as described in chapter 1. The sample includes all nonstudent, nonretired men aged twenty-one to sixty-five (inclusive) who had complete time use reports.

Table 3-4C reports the allocation of time for "other" nonemployed men, that is, men who did not report being employed, unemployed, or disabled. (Recall that students and retirees are not included in the sample.) This is the residual group of men whose reason for nonemployment is not explicitly included in the ATUS coding. The average leisure for this category is 130.5 hours per week, which is in between that of unemployed and that of disabled men. However, when education level is taken into account, the leisure gap between less- and more-educated "other" nonemployed men is roughly ten hours per week, which is greater than the gaps for either the unemployed or the disabled. This ten-hour gap is accommodated in part by a nearly five-hour-per-week difference in the sum of nonmarket work; gardening, lawn care, and pet care; and child care. The remaining five-hour difference occurs because the less-educated "other" nonemployed spent less time per week on informal market work, job search, their own medical care, religious and civic activities, and activities lumped into the "other" time use category.

To gain some perspective on the time allocation patterns reported in tables 3-3A, 3-3B, 3-3C, 3-4A, 3-4B, and 3-4C, we explore how men of different educational attainment in 2003–2005 allocated the time freed up by nonemployment.[13] Specifically, consider that less-educated employed men spent a total of forty-five hours per week on employment, training, and job search (table 3-3B). The corresponding number for more-educated employed men is forty-seven hours per week. What fraction of this forty-five or forty-seven hours per week did unemployed, disabled, and other nonemployed men allocate to leisure? What fractions did they allocate to nonmarket production, child care, medical care, and so on? To start, the difference in leisure between less-educated employed men and less-educated unemployed men is twenty-four hours per week, which accounts for roughly 53 percent of the additional available time. A large portion of the remaining twenty-one hours was spent on nonmarket work (19 percent), child care (4 percent), and civic, religious, and other activities (6 percent). The corresponding shares for more-educated unemployed men compared with more-educated working men are 48 percent for leisure and 18 percent for nonmarket work, while gardening, yard work, and pet care account for nearly 6 percent of the additional time.

Performing the same exercise for less- and more-educated disabled men reveals a slightly different picture. In particular, less-educated disabled men spent 90 percent of their additional forty-five hours per week on increased leisure. Another 8 percent of the additional time was spent on medical care and care for other adults. More-educated disabled men spent 87 percent of their additional time on leisure and 8.5 percent on their own medical care. These data show that almost all of the additional time available to the disabled in 2003–2005 was spent on leisure and health care, regardless of educational attainment.

4

Decomposing Leisure Differences: How Much Is Due to Employment Status?

The fact that less-educated men enjoyed more leisure during a period in which their employment rates fell raises the question of how much of the difference in leisure between less- and more-educated men is due to differences in employment status. In particular, it may be the case that some—or all—of the difference in leisure between groups with differing educational attainments is due to involuntary unemployment or disability. In this chapter we address this question by quantifying how much of the differences in time allocated to leisure seen between less- and more-educated men is attributable to employment status. We first look at the differences between less- and more-educated men at a point in time. We do this separately for 1985 and 2003–2005. We then consider the change in time allocation within a given education group over the period bracketed by those years. We do this separately for less- and for more-educated men.

To begin, consider the 1985 cross-section. From table 3-2A, less-educated men consumed 2.2 more hours of total leisure per week than did more-educated men. From table 3-1, the share of less-educated men employed in 1985 was 89 percent, 5 percentage points lower than the employment rate of more-educated men. The fact that employed men have less time for leisure suggests that some of the 2.2-hour leisure difference is due to this difference in employment rates. To see exactly how much, we use the data from tables 3-2B and 3-2C. In table 3-2B, we see that more-educated men who were employed in 1985 enjoyed 103.5 hours of leisure per week, whereas in table 3-2C, more-educated nonemployed men in that year consumed 130.0 hours per week. The difference across employment states for more-educated men is therefore 26.5 hours per week. Now consider a hypothetical 4-percentage-point decrease in more-educated men's employment rate, bringing it to the rate for less-educated men in 1985; this would increase leisure for the more-educated men by 0.04 x 26.5 = 1.3 hours per week. This represents 59 percent of the 2.2-hour difference in leisure time (1.3/2.2 = 0.59).

The remaining 41 percent (or 0.9 hour per week) is due to the fact that, in 1985, nonemployed men with less education consumed 134.6 hours of leisure per week, while nonemployed men with more education consumed 130.0 hours per week (table 3-2C). That is, conditional on employment status, less-educated men consumed an additional 0.9 hour of leisure per week in 1985, and their lower employment rate contributed an additional 1.3 hours per week.

We now perform the same exercise for 2003–2005. In that period less-educated men consumed 109.8 hours per week of leisure, while more-educated men consumed 102.3 hours per week, for a difference of 7.5 hours per week (table 3-3A). More-educated men had a 9-percentage-point advantage in employment rates (table 3-1) in 2003. In 2003–2005 more-educated nonemployed men consumed 26.8 hours per week more leisure than did more-educated employed men (tables 3-3A and 3-3B). We can therefore attribute 0.09 x 26.8 = 2.4 hours per week to differences in employment status, or 32 percent of the total difference of 7.5 hours per week.

The remaining 68 percent (5.1 hours per week) is due to differences that are *conditional* on employment status. In 2003–2005, for example, less-educated nonemployed men consumed 137.1 hours per week of leisure, while more-educated nonemployed men consumed 126.9 hours per week (table 3-3C). Moreover, less-educated employed men consumed 4.1 hours more leisure than more-educated employed men. These differences account for the majority— as much as two-thirds—of the 7.5-hour-per-week leisure gap between less- and more-educated men in 2003–2005. Thus, although the increased joblessness of the less educated is significant, it is not the only (or even the major) factor in explaining why less-educated men spent more time in leisure in 2003–2005 than their more-educated counterparts.

We now turn to the fact that less-educated men increased their leisure between 1985 and 2003–2005, while more-educated men decreased theirs (table 2-2). How much of this change over time is due to changing employment rates within each education group? We begin with less-educated men. They consumed 107.4 hours per week of leisure in 1985 and 109.8 hours per week in 2003–2005 (table 3-2A and table 3-3A), for an increase (with rounding) of 2.5 hours per week. Over the same period, employment rates for less-educated men fell from 89 percent in 1985 to 83 percent in 2003–2005 (table 3-1), a decline of 6 percentage points. What would their time allocation look like if this decline had not happened? In 2003–2005, less-educated nonemployed men consumed 33 hours per week more leisure than less-educated employed men (137.1 compared with 104.1 hours per week, from tables 3-3C and 3-3B, respectively). Therefore, the 6-percentage-point decline in their employment contributed 0.06 x 33 = 2.0 hours per week of additional leisure. This is 82 percent (with rounding) of their total 2.5-hour-per-week increase in leisure. Therefore, most of the increase in leisure for less-educated men between 1985 and 2003–2005 can be attributed to the decline in employment rates for this group.

On the other hand, more-educated men reduced their total leisure time over this period. In 1985 these men enjoyed 105.1 hours per week of leisure, whereas in 2003–2005 they consumed 102.3 hours per week, for a decline of 2.8 hours per week (table 3-2A and table 3-3A). Over this same period their employment rate fell 2 percentage points, from 94 percent to 92 percent (table 3-1). That is, more-educated men reduced their leisure at the same time that they reduced their employment rates. To decompose their 2.8-hour-per-week decline in leisure, consider the fact that in 2003–2005, more-educated employed men consumed 100.1 hours per week of leisure, while their nonemployed counterparts consumed 126.9 hours per week (tables 3-3B and 3-3C, respectively), for a difference of 26.8 hours per week. A decline in their employment rate of 2 percentage points would therefore predict 0.02 x 26.8 = 0.5 hour per week of additional leisure. That is, all else equal, the decline in the employment rate for more-educated men contributed an increase of leisure of about 0.5 hour per week. The fact that leisure actually declined for more-educated men is therefore attributable to the declines within employment status. In particular, employed educated men consumed 103.5 hours per week of leisure in 1985 (table 3-2B), but only 100.1 hours per week in 2003–2005 (table 3-3B), for a decline within employment status of 3.4 hours per week. As also seen from these two tables, the increased work performed by more-educated employed men is being done at home in the form of more child care and care of other adults, as well as in more gardening, yard work, and pet care. Similarly, nonemployed educated men reduced their leisure by roughly 3 hours per week over the same period (table 3-2C and table 3-3C). These changes explain more than 100 percent of the 2.8-percentage-point decline in leisure of more-educated men between 1985 and 2003–2005. Therefore, while more-educated men slightly reduced their rate of employment, they dramatically changed how they allocate their time both while employed and while not employed.

Taken together, these results suggest that although employment status is important in understanding the leisure differentials that exist between less- and more-educated men in 2003–2005, it is not the sole (or even the predominant) force. Increased nonemployment (from both unemployment and disability) explains most of the increase in leisure of less-educated men. However, changes in employment status do not alone explain why the educational leisure gap has increased so much, given that none of the significant changes in more-educated men's leisure are attributable to changing employment status.

A final calculation reinforces this point. As we have seen, less-educated men increased their leisure by 2.5 hours per week between 1985 and 2003–2005, while more-educated men reduced their leisure by 2.8 hours per week; together these changes generated an increase in the leisure gap between the two groups of 5.3 hours per week. We found above that employment status predicted an increase in the educational leisure gap of 1.1 hours per week, from 1.3 to 2.4 hours per week. This is 21 percent of the observed change of 5.3 hours per week. Similarly, if we use our second set of calculations, changes in employment status predict that less-educated men would have increased their leisure between 1985 and 2003–2005 by 2.0 hours per week, and that more-educated men would have increased theirs by 0.5 hour per week. This implies a change in the educational leisure gap of 1.5 hours per week (2.0 minus 0.5), or 28 percent. In either case, the rising nonemployment of less-educated men is not the predominant component of the increasing leisure gap between less- and more-educated men. If changes in employment status do not explain the increased leisure gap, what does? We answer this question in the next chapter.

5

Discussion and Conclusion

In this chapter we offer some concluding thoughts and interpretations pertaining to our results.

Interpreting Trends in Leisure Inequality

The facts presented above do not fit easily into standard economic models. To recap, we observed that less-educated individuals increased their leisure relative to more-educated individuals during a period when the relative wages of the less-educated workers fell. In other words, when you make less, you work less. In a simple model of labor supply, one would be tempted to interpret this finding as evidence that the substitution effect of wages dominates the income effect. That is, the lower wage deters employment more than the resulting lower income encourages it. However, this does not explain the changes in leisure conditional on nonemployment. Moreover, it does not accord with why leisure increased uniformly as wages increased uniformly between 1965 and 1985.

The fact that the time allocation of the less-educated nonemployed has changed so dramatically, both relative to their counterparts in 1985 and relative to the more-educated nonemployed, also raises interesting questions. Again, as this subsample is not employed, it cannot simply reflect labor supply decisions. It may, however, represent changes in the relative price of leisure. For example, the dramatic rise in television watching coincided with a large increase in the number of shows produced (a change that can also be interpreted as a sharp decline in the price of quality-adjusted entertainment). Such movements in relative prices may be an important driving force of the trends in time use. However, this explanation does not tell us why more-educated individuals did not respond equally to this decline in price.

One possible explanation of the unequal response is that the preference for leisure (the disutility of work) increased more for low-educated workers during this time. This explanation is consistent with the fact that individuals of differing educational attainment who are out of the labor market and facing the same prices exhibit dramatically different time allocation decisions.

Welfare Implications of Leisure Inequality

The results documented in this monograph raise important questions regarding the interpretation of changing inequality in the United States between individuals of different educational attainment. How does one weigh the relative growth of leisure for the less educated against the simultaneous decline in their relative wages, consumption, and market hours? To gain some insight into this question, start with a simple benchmark. Suppose market wages differ exogenously across individuals. Suppose also that workers can freely choose how many hours they want to work in the labor market. Depending on the income and substitution elasticities of labor supply with respect to wages, higher wages may result in either more or fewer market hours worked, and consequently either more or less leisure may be consumed. Nevertheless, we have enough information to say that the high-wage workers are better off: they can always choose the same time allocation as low-wage workers and still enjoy more consumption (same hours worked, but at higher wages). In this simple benchmark, the hourly market wage is sufficient to rank outcomes: even if preferences differ across individuals, the same individual will always prefer the higher wage to the lower wage.

That less-educated workers enjoyed more leisure in 2003–2005 even though they were working the same number of market hours as the more-educated workers suggests there may be more to the story. Less-educated workers spend less than do more-educated workers. Because the return to home production is higher for these workers, they have the incentive to augment their consumption by shopping intensively, preparing their meals themselves, and doing their own home repairs. Conversely, with a low level of market inputs, diminishing returns to home production will set in more quickly for less-educated households. This makes the prediction of how much home production less-educated individuals should perform relative to more-educated individuals (conditional on the same level of market work) theoretically ambiguous.

Nevertheless, the fact that less-educated people always devote less time than more-educated people to home production, civic and religious activities, and child care whether they are employed or nonemployed suggests that they may simply prefer leisure to consumption. In particular, less-educated workers may value leisure time over higher expenditure relatively more than do more-educated workers. In this case, workers will optimally choose differing levels of human capital (both that acquired through education and that acquired through on-the-job training) subject to constraints on liquidity and ability. This raises the question of to what extent the lower wages offered to less-educated workers reflect endogenous choices regarding human capital acquisition as well as exogenous (to the worker) market forces. The results documented in this monograph suggest that heterogeneity in the relative value of market goods and free time—and the consequent effects on human capital and wages—may be a fruitful framework for improving our understanding of income inequality.

Concluding Caveats

We acknowledge some key difficulties in measuring time allocation across people and over time. One major issue is the definition of leisure. Cooking may be leisure for one person and work for another, and the same can be said for yard work, vehicle repair, shopping, and so on. Our research, therefore, has taken a relatively agnostic approach. However, the leisure patterns documented in this manuscript can be seen most clearly in one category, namely, watching television. Compared with most other activities, this activity seems unambiguously to be one of leisure, and its importance in determining the trends in total leisure therefore provides some confidence regarding the impact of misclassification of activities into or out of leisure. Further, we do not address leisure on the job (e.g., extended coffee breaks or surfing the Internet in one's office) or during retirement. Considering the amount of time that Americans today spend in retirement (given longer life spans), the results presented here underestimate the increases in leisure over the last half century. However, if leisure on the job differs markedly over time by education category, this poses an important—but hard to measure—caveat to our results.

Appendix

We used the following time use surveys: the 1965–1966 Americans' Use of Time survey, the 1985 Americans' Use of Time survey, and the 2003, 2004, and 2005 waves of the American Time Use Survey. All of the data, codebooks, and programs used to create the time use categories for this monograph are available on our data webpage (troi.cc.rochester.edu/~maguiar/timeuse_data/datapage.html).

The programs on the data webpage include a detailed description of how we took the raw data from each of the time use surveys and created consistent measures for each of the time use categories across the different surveys. The classification used in this manuscript is the same as that in Aguiar and Hurst (2007a), except that in this analysis we broke out time spent in gardening, lawn care, and pet care as a separate category. In our prior work we had included this category in our measures of nonmarket work and leisure.

All time use surveys that we analyzed used a twenty-four-hour recall of the previous day's activities to record time diary information. The 1965–1966 Americans' Use of Time survey was conducted by the Survey Research Center at the University of Michigan. The survey sampled one individual per household in 2,001 households in which at least one adult person between the ages of nineteen and sixty-five was employed in a nonfarm occupation during the previous year. This survey does not contain sampling weights, so we weighted each respondent equally (before adjusting for the day of week of each diary). Of the 2,001 individuals, 776 came from Jackson, Michigan. The time use data were obtained by having respondents keep a complete diary of their activities for a single twenty-four-hour period between November 15 and December 15,

TABLE A-1

ACTIVITIES INCLUDED IN TIME USE CATEGORIES

Time use category	Examples of activities included
Total market work (exc. job search)	Work for pay at main job, work for pay at other jobs (including work in the informal sector), commuting to/from work, meals/breaks at work
Job search	Searching for a job, going on job interviews, preparing resume
Education	Taking classes for degree, taking personal interest courses, homework for coursework, research for coursework
Home and vehicle maintenance	Vehicle repair, outdoor home repair, outdoor home painting, outdoor home maintenance
Obtaining goods and services	Grocery shopping, shopping for other goods, comparison shopping, clipping coupons, going to bank, going to post office, meeting with lawyer, going to veterinarian (category excludes any time spent acquiring medical care)
All other home production	Food preparation, food presentation, cleanup after meals, washing/drying clothes, ironing, dusting, vacuuming, indoor home cleaning, indoor home painting
Child care	Primary child care (e.g., breastfeeding, changing diapers), educational child care (e.g., reading to children, helping with homework), recreational child care (e.g., playing games with children, going to zoo with children)
Gardening, pet care, lawn care	Caring for lawn, gardening, care of houseplants, playing with pets, caring for pets
Television	Watching television
Socializing	Attending/hosting social events, playing indoor games, telephone calls
Exercise and sport	Playing sports, attending sporting events, exercising
Reading	Reading books and magazines, reading personal mail, reading personal e-mail
Hobbies and other entertainment	Arts and crafts, collecting, playing musical instrument, going to movies and theater, listening to music, computer use for leisure
Eating	Eating meals at home, eating meals away from home
Sleeping	Sleeping, napping
Personal care	Grooming, bathing, sex, going to the bathroom (category excludes any time spent on one's own medical care)
Own medical care	Visiting doctor's/dentist's office (including time waiting), dressing wounds, taking medicine
Care of other adults	Taking care of elderly parents or grandparents, caring for a sick friend

Table A-1 continued

Time use category	Examples of activities included
Religious and civic activities	Religious practice/participation, participation in fraternal organizations, volunteer work, union meetings, Alcoholics Anonymous meetings
Other	Time spent on activities the respondent is unwilling to detail or cannot remember, unclassified travel and security procedures related to travel, activities that do not fall under the primary classification categories

1965, or between March 7 and April 29, 1966. In our analysis we included the Jackson, Michigan, sample.

The 1985 Americans' Use of Time survey was conducted by the Survey Research Center at the University of Maryland. The sample of 4,939 individuals was nationally representative with respect to adults over the age of eighteen living in homes with at least one telephone. The survey sampled its respondents from January 1985 through December 1985.

The American Time Use Survey is conducted by the U.S. Bureau of Labor Statistics (BLS). Participants in ATUS, which includes children over the age of fifteen, are drawn from the existing sample of the Current Population Survey. The individual is sampled approximately three months after completion of the final CPS survey. At the time of the ATUS survey, the BLS updates the respondent's employment and demographic information. The ATUS waves totaled 20,720, 13,973, and 13,039 respondents in 2003, 2004, and 2005, respectively.

We restricted our sample to include only those individuals from each survey between the ages of twenty-one and sixty-five who were neither retired nor students and who had a complete twenty-four-hour time diary, including entries for age, education, work status, sex, and the presence of a child in the household. This last restriction was relevant for only 11 individuals in 1965 and 118 individuals in 1985. The restriction that all individuals had to have a complete time diary was also innocuous. Only 43 individuals in 1965 and 3 individuals in 1985 had a time diary in which total time

TABLE A-2
DESCRIPTIVE STATISTICS FOR TIME USE SAMPLES

Variable	1965	1985	2003–2005
Age (years)	40.3	39.2	41.3
Sex			
Men	45%	44%	49%
Education level: men			
<12 years	36%	13%	12%
=12 years	34%	42%	32%
13–15 years	14%	16%	26%
≥16 years	16%	29%	0.30%
Education level: women			
<12 years	32%	13%	10%
=12 years	44%	48%	31%
13–15 years	14%	17%	29%
≥16 years	10%	22%	30%
Family statistics			
Married	82%	69%	63%
With children	63%	43%	46%
Average no. of children per couple	1.6	0.8	0.9

SOURCE: Authors' calculations from data in the Americans' Use of Time surveys and the American Time Use Surveys.
NOTE: See the data appendix for a description of the sample and Table 1 for the relevant sample sizes.

across all activities summed to a number other than twenty-four hours. In total, our sample included 1,854 individuals from 1965, 3,115 individuals from 1985, and 34,697 individuals from 2003–2005.

One challenge in comparing the time use data sets with each other is that the surveys report time use using differing levels of aggregation. In particular, the categories used in the ATUS are very different from those in the earlier surveys (which had activity categories similar to each other). For example, each survey before the

2003–2005 ATUS includes roughly ninety different subcategories of individual time use. The 2003–2005 surveys include over four hundred different subcategories of individual time use.

To create consistent measures of time use over time and across the surveys, we worked with the raw data at the level of subcategories. To render our analysis tractable and to lessen classification issues across the surveys, we aggregated an individual's time allocation into the twenty broad categories described in table A-1. Travel time associated with each activity is included in the total time spent on the activity.

The raw time use data in each of the surveys are reported in units of "minutes per day" (totaling 1,440 minutes a day). We converted the minutes-per-day reports to hours per week. When presenting the averages from the time use data within each demographic cell, we weighted the data using the sampling weights within each of the time use surveys. The weights account for differential response rates to ensure that the samples are nationally representative. We also adjusted weights so that each day of the week and each survey are equally represented. See Aguiar and Hurst (2007a) for a full description.

Notes

1. The final three categories—eating, sleeping, and personal care—have both personal maintenance qualities as well as potential leisure attributes. However, none of the results in this monograph hinge on the inclusion of these three categories. To drive this point home, we report the trends for each of the separate leisure subcomponents in most of the analysis that follows. For a full description of trends in leisure excluding eating, sleeping, and personal care, see Aguiar and Hurst (2007a).

2. Our work adds to the existing literature on measuring changes in the allocation of time. In Aguiar and Hurst (2007a), we document an increase in leisure for the average individual between 1965 and 2003. Our discussion in chapter 2 is based on this earlier work. In addition, three classic book-length references have also examined trends in the allocation of time during earlier periods: Ghez and Becker (1975), Juster and Stafford (1985), and Robinson and Godbey (1999). The last two books also documented an increase in leisure for the average individual during the periods they analyzed. Schor (1992) is a popular, and controversial, study that draws different conclusions about the trends in leisure between the mid-1960s and the early 1980s.

3. Time spent collecting unemployment benefits is *not* included in job search time but as a component of civic activities.

4. See Aguiar and Hurst (2007a) for an analysis of different definitions of leisure. The coding for *eating at work* has changed across surveys, an issue discussed at length in the robustness appendix to Aguiar and Hurst (2007a). See troi.cc.rochester.edu/~maguiar/timeuse_data/robustness_appendix.pdf.

5. Specifically, we look at demographic cells defined by certain attributes, such as age, family status, sex, educational attainment, and employment status. When we report demographically adjusted differences, we construct cells defined by age and family status within each education category. We distinguish single households from married households and households that include children (regardless of marital status), thus separating multiperson households from single-person households. Given the

small sample size in 1985 in some of the subcategories, we do not distinguish households by number of children.

6. We also performed the analysis retaining retirees in the sample. The main results are qualitatively unchanged, although the magnitudes with respect to the overall increase in leisure between 1985 and 2003 are smaller (particularly for the less-educated households). The reason is that the increase in disability programs in the United States may have induced marginal older workers to classify themselves as disabled in recent periods rather than as retired.

7. The 1965 survey sample was drawn from households where at least one person was employed during the previous year. This potentially biases the employment rates upward. However, the reported employment rates for men in the 1965 sample do not differ markedly from those in the nationally representative 1968 PSID. This issue is discussed in the appendix of Aguiar and Hurst (2007a).

8. Each line in the figure is the kernel estimate of the probability density over leisure time in the corresponding sample, with the total area under the line integrating to 1.

9. We note that the significant differences in labor force *entry* for women of different educational attainment are the primary force behind the leisure gap among women, a phenomenon related to the pattern for men due to the prominence of differences in market labor trends. We leave the examination of the gap in leisure among women to future research.

10. Trends in labor market participation by educational attainment have been documented by others. For example, see Juhn, Murphy, and Topel (2002).

11. Specifically, we use whether the respondents reported disability in response to a question of whether they had held a job in the last seven days, as well as responses to such questions as "Last month you were reported to have a disability. Does your disability prevent you from doing any kind of work for the next six months?"

12. The leisure subcategories are not exhaustive. There is an "other" leisure category, which we omit from the table.

13. Hamermesh and Donald (2007) undertake a similar exercise to estimate the fixed costs of employment.

References

Aguiar, Mark, and Erik Hurst. 2005. "Consumption vs. Expenditure." *Journal of Political Economy* 113 (5): 919–48.

_____. 2007a. "Measuring Trends in Leisure: The Allocation of Time Over Five Decades." *Quarterly Journal of Economics* 122 (3): 969–1006.

_____. 2007b. "Lifecycle Prices and Production." *American Economic Review* (forthcoming).

Attanasio, Orazio, Erich Battistin, and Hidehiko Ichimura (2004). "What Really Happened to Consumption Inequality in the US?" NBER Working Paper 10338.

Attanasio, Orazio, and Steve Davis. 1996. "Relative Wage Movements and the Distribution of Consumption." *Journal of Political Economy* 104 (6): 1227–62.

Autor, David, and Mark Duggan. 2003. "The Rise in the Disability Rolls and the Decline in Unemployment." *Quarterly Journal of Economics* 118 (1): 157–206.

Becker, Gary. 1965. "A Theory of the Allocation of Time." *Economic Journal* 75: 493–517.

Ghez, Gilbert, and Gary Becker. 1975. *The Allocation of Time and Goods over the Life Cycle.* New York: Columbia University Press.

Greenwood, Jeremy, Ananth Seshadri, and Mehmet Yorukoglu. 2005. "Engines of Liberation." *Review of Economic Studies* 72 (1): 109–33.

Hamermesh, Daniel, and Stephen Donald. 2007. "The Time and Timing Costs of Market Work." Working Paper 13127. Cambridge, Mass.: National Bureau of Economic Research.

Juhn, Chinhui, Kevin Murphy, and Robert Topel. 2002. "Current Unemployment, Historically Contemplated." *Brookings Papers on Economic Activity*, no. 1: 79–116.

Juster, Thomas, and Frank Stafford. 1985. "Time Goods and Well-Being." Ann Arbor, Mich.: Institute for Social Research, University of Michigan.

Katz, Lawrence, and David Autor. 1999. "Changes in the Wage Structure and Earnings Inequality." In *Handbook of Labor Economics*, vol. 3A, ed. Orley Ashenfelter and David Card. Oxford, U.K.: Elsevier Science.

Krueger, Dirk, and Fabrizio Perri. 2006. "Does Income Inequality Lead to Consumption Inequality? Evidence and Theory." *Review of Economic Studies* 73 (1): 163–93.

Reid, Margaret. 1934. *Economics of Household Production.* New York: John Wiley and Sons.

Robinson, John, and Geoffrey Godbey. 1999. *Time for Life.* University Park, Pa.: Pennsylvania State University Press.

Schor, Juliet. 1992. *The Overworked American: The Unexpected Decline of Leisure.* New York: Basic Books.

About the Authors

Mark Aguiar is an associate professor of economics at the University of Rochester. He is a research associate for the National Bureau of Economic Research and an associate editor for the *Review of Economic Dynamics*, and serves on the board of editors for the *American Economic Journal: Macroeconomics*. Professor Aguiar's interests span a number of fields, including the study of life-cycle consumption and savings, the interplay of time allocation and consumption, trends in time allocation, current account dynamics, sovereign debt, emerging market business cycles, and growth. His research has appeared in top economic journals, including the *American Economic Review*, the *Journal of Political Economy*, the *Review of Economic Studies*, and the *Quarterly Journal of Economics*. Professor Aguiar received the 2006 TIAA-CREF Paul Samuelson Award for best published paper dealing with household financial security for "Consumption vs. Expenditure" (co-authored with Erik Hurst, *Journal of Political Economy*, October 2005). Previously, he served in the U.S. Foreign Service, with postings in Korea and China as well as at the Department of State in Washington, D.C. Professor Aguiar received an undergraduate degree in history from Brown University and a PhD in economics from MIT.

Erik Hurst is the V. Duane Rath Professor of Economics and the Neubauer Family Faculty Fellow at the University of Chicago, Booth School of Business, where he has been a member of the faculty since 1999. Professor Hurst serves as a research associate for the National Bureau of Economic Research and is an associate editor of the *American Economic Journal: Macroeconomics*. His research focuses on macroeconomic policy, household consumption behavior, time use, entrepreneurship, and household financial behavior. Professor Hurst's work has appeared in several leading economic journals, including the *American Economic Review*, the *Journal of Political Economy*, and the *Quarterly Journal of Economics*. He received the 2006 TIAA-CREF Paul Samuelson Award for best published paper dealing with household financial security for "Consumption vs. Expenditure" (co-authored with Mark Aguiar, *Journal of Political Economy*, October 2005). Professor Hurst earned a bachelor's degree in economics from Clarkson University in 1993. He went on to earn a master's degree in economics (1993) and a PhD in economics (1999) from the University of Michigan.